Walking the Heartroad:
The Devotional Path for Spirit-Workers

Silence Maestas

Walking
the
Heartroad

*The Devotional Path
for Spirit-Workers*

Silence Maestas

Hubbardston, Massachusetts

Asphodel Press
12 Simond Hill Road
Hubbardston, MA 01452

Walking the Heartroad: The Devotional Path for Spirit-Workers
© 2008 Silence Maestas
ISBN 978-0-615-26215-4

Printed in cooperation with
Lulu Enterprises, Inc.
860 Aviation Parkway, Suite 300
Morrisville, NC 27560

For Loki, mi corazon…

Acknowledgements

I am indebted to all those who have shared their devotional journeys with me over the years; their example and influence have enriched my own devotional practice in countless ways. Further gratitude belongs to Abby Helasdottir for her beautiful cover art and to the people who read and offered feedback on early versions of this book.

Most importantly, I am grateful to all the deities in my life, past and present. It is Their love that has inspired this book; They have taught me everything I know about the Heartroad and walk it together with me. My thanks and love belong especially to Loki and Hela, whose patience and love have exceeded anything I could have imagined. Thank you.

Contents

Introduction: About This Book..*i*

Part 1: The Heartroad

Examining the Road.. 1

Walking Together.. 5

Finding a Form 17

Part 2: Forging the Tool

Bumps in the Road.. 27

Love Comes Full Circle 33

Epilogue: Lilahava... *37*

Introduction: About This Book

Love, dedication, desire, service, commitment, and longing—these are all characteristic of a devotional life, one lived in the midst of a passionate relationship with the divine, with the spirits that surround us, with the self, and with the world. This is a rare path, and it is a rare person who chooses to walk it. Living a life that focuses on bringing the worlds together requires emotional stamina and fortitude, as well as the willingness to change oneself for the sake of greater things. Both the sacrifices and the rewards made on the devotional path are great, and they allow the devotee to continue the work that leads them inexorably into the arms of the Divine.

Devotional practice is the art of religious love. Many people would describe the feelings they have for their Gods as "love", but few can actually say that they are in love with Them. Few can call their beloved deities Mother or Father and not feel it to be purely metaphor. Few people relate to the divine as a master teacher, as an exacting mistress, or as a child loved without reservation. Devotional mysticism makes the Gods and spirits distinctly personal. Their presence becomes a constant in one's life, and this knowledge is carried out into the world, forever altering the way the devotee encounters all aspects of their life. The worlds become blurred—the spirits peer from every corner and the voices of the Gods infuse daily life. Through love, the worlds mix and mingle.

When an individual is contacted by the Gods and/or spirits to do a specific kind of work, and establishes ongoing two-way communication with them, we call them spirit-workers. Spirit-work is service and effort dedicated to the unseen world; this may be accomplished by aiding the spirits, a human community, or both. Their service may be approached through personal commitment or involuntary compulsion, but either way the spirit-worker is forced to live in more than one world at once, forever mindful of the effect they have on each.

A spirit-worker's distinction, as such, varies in time and space. The term itself is entirely new, coined to describe a collective set of unusual phenomena that alters a person's life in such a way that they can never fully back out of it and go back to living unaware. Many cultures describe their spiritual functionaries as being compelled by the spirits; if these demands are ignored, the functionary is punished with madness or even death. In serving the spirits and Gods, and by seeing to the spiritual needs of their immediate community, this functionary straddles the shifting boundary between the worlds. They live on the edge, not fully part of one world or the other.

Mystics also live in two worlds, though many have sought to reject the physical world in favor of the spiritual. They practice austerities to discipline their body and mind in order to be made into a vessel fit for divine inspiration. Some mystics were and are renunciates, removing themselves from the distractions of the world in order to focus singly on their God. Some mystics immerse themselves in the world, wanting to see their beloved in every surface and reflected back in every face they encounter.

Some attempts have been made to firmly demarcate the boundaries between devotional practice, mysticism, and spirit-work. For myself, as someone who touches all three realms, these arguments have served only to limit my experience of the numinous. In my experience, spirits and deities are too complex to be held in place by semantics, and love and service are too infinite to be confined by human distinctions. The titles bestowed by my personal beloveds are the true markers of power for me, and in my mind should be placed above the labels that humans chose to share or withhold.

There can be mysticism and love in spirit-work. These three things intertwine, blend, and combine to form a unique expression of service and devotion. When these paths blend effectively, efforts are given to the spirits without grudge, motivated by compassion instead of obligation. Aid is given to humanity out of love for the Gods and for this world. The devotional path shapes spirit-work into a romance between two worlds.

This book is specifically about the devotional life of spirit-work, as I have experienced it. It is gleaned from my personal devotional life, which has been shaped by spirit-work, and from observing the lives of people I have come into contact with along the way. There's no way that my life can speak to every spirit-worker, or to every person who might become a spirit-worker. For example, I can't begin to encompass the experience of those people who love their Gods but who don't have the two-way connection of spirit-work. Even though this book talks about spirit-work a great deal (and about a particular variety of spirit-work, at that), it is to those people who are passionately in love relationship with their Gods and spirits that I most wish to speak.

This is a book about love, about perseverance, about strength, and about service. In it are a few of the valuable lessons this life has given me. It is representational of only a small moment in time, just one step on my long path. I offer it with the hope that it can act as a roadmap to someone who is beginning to explore—or someone who is a seasoned citizen of—the wild landscapes of the heart. I'm fascinated by love, particularly the love we have for our Gods, for the spirits around us, and for religion. Devotional mysticism called to me from a very young age, and after bumbling around in my birth religion for several years, I hit on paganism as a teenager and finally fell in love. I began my first deliberate steps on the Heartroad and never looked back.

Mysticism, including devotional practice and spirit-work, might be called the dream life of a religion—intangible, irrational, and completely personal. In this analogy, the waking life of a religion includes everything giving that religion structure—the tangible, rational, quantifiable parts of faith: doctrine, ritual, dogma, law, and history. All this is vitally important to a religion, but structure without spirit is only half the story.

Psychology tells us that dreaming is essential to a healthy psyche, so perhaps the dream life of a religion is essential to a religion's health, as well. Our spiritual dreams are everything not bound by doctrine or history, those parts of faith that call to our deepest hearts, that inspire ecstasy and smash preconceptions. Just as everyone dreams whether they are aware of it or not, everyone who strives for religious experience has a mystical life. Something called them to their religion of choice and something keeps bringing them back. Mysticism cannot be separated from the true practice of any religion.

Without the dreams of mysticism, religion is only a set of rules and a collection of stories. Mysticism is personal and completely irrational, just like dreams are. This irrational, uncontrollable element is naturally threatening to those who are heavily invested in maintaining the ironclad rules that govern their faith, especially when an individual's mystical experience goes beyond what small measure is expected. People who believe in keeping the deities at arm's length, or who want to regulate the interaction of deities and humans, or who give lip service to the spirits while believing that spirits are lesser beings become very angry when their treasured ideas are thrown into disarray. Someone claiming to be close to the Gods, or who desires to be so, may be reminded that Gods only speak to heroes and kings; the person who hears the spirits will be ridiculed into silence, and the person whose dealings with the Gods refuses to be confined to holy days alone has always been under a cloud of suspicion.

What these nay-sayers may forget is that religion itself is, by definition, something that has to be taken on faith. Religion is not rational, explainable, predictable, logical, or tidy; face it, no one has yet been able to logically prove the existence of the Gods. There can't be religion without faith in something—some deity, some uniting force, some greater purpose that drives the universe. None of these beliefs can be rationally justified except by logic intrinsic to the religion that is justifying itself. And I believe that's okay. I don't want my religion to be rational! I have to be rational in the rest of my life, why not give me an arena where I can think with my heart as well as my head? What harm comes from personally experiencing those deities I love?

No harm may come from it ... but accountability does, and perhaps that's what scares people away from deeper levels of mysticism. The mystic hears the voices of the Gods and accountability is placed into their trembling hands. The spirits know where to find them. The

Gods know their name. The mystic must now be accountable for their actions, and aware that what they do and say has a greater affect on the world than they previously realized. This is a grave gift. If the mystic accepts their experience as reality (and not everyone does) then they are held to a greater standard and have to take responsibility. The awareness of responsibility is one facet of Right Action so, to keep in step with Right Action, the mystic now has to behave in a way that benefits the world, or at least does the smallest harm. This awareness is a difficult thing to become adjusted to in a culture seemingly obsessed with passing the buck, but it can be done. (If I can correct some of my bad habits, believe me, anyone can do it.)

The rewards for living with greater mindfulness are as rich as the responsibilities. The world becomes at once much larger and much smaller than it was before; small actions have real results, and are part of a chain of actions that stretch off into infinity. Living with awareness makes me feel like an active participant in my life; life becomes what *I* choose and a feeling of greater ownership results. Inside that greater ownership comes the knowledge that I am not an isolated entity living alone in a cold, uncaring world. I am connected to the spirits, and they to me. I am connected to the deities, and They walk with me. I am connected to this world, to other people, and to ourselves. I am not separate from any part of this world and, as I love myself, I come to love the world. In the end, it always comes back to love.

This book, then, is my gift to spirit-workers. It is the map of my devotion, and how I came to find joy in this path. If my footsteps on this path are of use to you, take their road and may it bring you joy.

Part 1:

The Heartroad

Examining the Road

Being drawn into spirit-work is an intense, transformative, life-changing experience. The spirits grab us from out of the blue, and the illusions we have about ourselves are rebuilt from visions of unflinching honesty. Learning to live this life is a little like falling in love—unexpected, unlooked for, and all-encompassing. Love and spirit-work go hand-in-hand for me. Both paths bring us to the heights and depths of emotional experience and ecstasy, force us to become more than who we believed ourselves to be, and demand that we become open to others as we become stronger in ourselves. We are not alone in these processes. Goddesses, Gods, and spirits are beside us on every step of the path, sometimes leading us forward, sometimes pushing us from behind. Often, it is love itself that shapes the form our spirit-work takes.

Devotion is at the heart of my life; the more I fall in love, the more I am drawn into spirit-work. Love, in its myriad forms, is the fuel that drives my practice, regardless of how that practice is expressed. Love is my motivation, my goal, and my achievement. Despite the fact that many other spirit-workers that I know are deeply involved in devotional work, we don't talk much about this love or how it shapes our work. Devotion is largely a private thing, part of the space shared between a person and their beloved deity (or deities); the prevailing opinion seems to be that, since devotion involves the private lives of people and Gods, it shouldn't be openly expressed. We may talk to trusted friends who are similarly devoted to their Gods, but spirit-workers on the whole don't talk about devotion or about the tools devotion gives us: compassion, love, humility, bravery, faith, and peace.

Some spirit-workers practice in traditions that have a clearly defined devotional path, while others do not. Those practicing in the pre-Christian tradition of northern Europe (like myself) may be at a loss about how to talk about their devotional practices, especially if they came to spirit-work from modern reconstructionist Norse religion. It is my firm opinion that the various branches of the Northern Tradition do have a native devotional path. The work I do inside the Norse reconstructionist community consistently leads me to believe this, but what is lacking is a vocabulary to describe these experiences; instead, people seem to merely take pot-shots at one another. I have noticed that many modern Norse religionists talk loudly and at length about their deities, but run the other direction when someone claims to be in close contact with Them or desires to be so. Devotion is often seen as a self-indulgent practice that doesn't benefit the larger community. However, devotional practices are found in traditions around the world; it would be absurd to assume that ancient Heathens never had intense devotional relationships with their deities. There are examples in ancient primary sources that demonstrate precisely this, and many modern Heathens certainly experience very personal relationships with their Gods, as do the spirit-workers who work in the Northern Tradition.

However, we aren't entirely without tools to help us talk about devotion. Most of the major religions of the world have a mystical tradition that is frequently rooted in its forms. Mystics throughout history have experienced the call of the divine and have sought to open themselves fully to that presence through renunciation, service, praise, or just through love. The rich mystic traditions of Hinduism, Islam, and Christianity give us some idea of the depth a devotional life can have. We can share in the ecstasy of Mirabai, Ramprasad, St. Teresa of Avila, and Rumi through the passionate writing they left us. Others have left us no legacy; those who serve selflessly are often forgotten, having only desired to empty themselves in order to be filled with their God. We can look at these traditions and see our unique lives reflected back.

But despite the devotional path being found in most religious traditions, it is often marginalized and even criticized. All mystic practices are subversive because mysticism takes an individual away from a structured tradition and allows them to see a part of life (and religion) that is hidden to most people. A person's relationship with the world is reformed by mystical practice. In *bhakti*, the Hindu devotional path, a mystic's *ishta devata* or chosen deity is seen in the whole world—animals, trees, buildings, and people all become a disguise of the Beloved. Whether or not mysticism is a capacity that all people have (or should have) is debatable, but what is known is that historically, only a handful of people seem to be called to the struggle of seeing the world anew.

Since spirit-work involves seeing the world in a way that is radically different than the way others see it—even others in our own religions—I tend to think of spirit-work as a form of mysticism. As such, it is not surprising that so many spirit-workers are involved in deep devotional relationships with deities and/or spirits. The roles that the spirits play in our lives remove illusion by forcing us to greater honesty—emotional honesty, honesty with others, and honesty with ourselves. Sometimes this journey is hard as we sacrifice one thing after another; what we treasure may be ripped from our lives by force, or we may be required to willingly abandon it. Sometimes this journey is sweet; we may be charmed or seduced away from a quiet, normal life until the only thing we desire is to smash anything that stands between us and our Beloved.

Our lives may not be made easier for the presence of the spirits, but they are richer. Love is not always an easy thing; we experience grief and deep loss on this path. Sorrow is a natural part of lives dedicated to service, and a devotional practice gives unique insight to suffering. The ups and downs of this path allow us to share the Gods with the world, and the things we gain from our unique relationships can belong to more people than just ourselves. Though I typically refer to deities alone, what I have to say about Gods and Goddesses applies equally to the spirits we love as well. Indeed, the line between God and spirit is blurred, subjective, and impossible to pin down.

Devotional practice can bring many important tools to spirit-work. Patience and perseverance are cultivated through repeated attention paid to the Gods, even in the times when They fall silent. Seeing the Gods as individuals, complete with Their failings and weaknesses, teaches us compassion. Attention is needed to constantly notice Their presence all around us. Honesty and self-knowledge are gained when we begin to see ourselves through Their eyes. Their presence inspires us to do and create things we might never have dreamed of attempting. We have to be brave to love without reserve and face those who would belittle and disregard what is most precious to us. Humility comes from serving others; spirit-work wields us as tools and devotion helps us become custom-fitted to Those we serve. Facing doubt and confusion with trust builds faith. The love and peace we find in being in the presence of our Gods can be turned outward for the benefit of those we encounter and aid. For those of us on the devotional path, spirit-work is not simply a private exercise that supports our other, more obvious jobs; on the other side, our devotion is central to our function and as such, benefits many more people than just ourselves.

Walking the Heartroad requires as much practice and skill as the rest of our work. It may be possible to find teachers to assist us in other aspects of our paths, or to use clues buried in ancient texts, and certainly support and validation can come from other people, providing valuable feedback in our work ... but in the end, the devotional path is solitary and our final teacher is the deit(ies) we love. They will guide, prod, and pull us toward this path, but They also require constant self-motivation. Making room for the Gods in our lives is a lifelong pursuit; it is a goal that motivates the choices we make, but is also affected by all the things we experience along the way.

Devotion is a powerful practice; ecstatic and deeply transformative. It creates revolutions in the heart and changes lives entirely. I have walked the devotional path for more than a decade and have witnessed its power in my life and in the lives of others. When you walk the Heartroad, everything you thought you knew about yourself will be rewritten until the only familiar thing in your life is the One you focus on. Devotion blurs the line between this world and the Otherworlds; in this liminal space deep magic can, and does, happen.

Walking Together

One of the characteristics that distinguishes spirit-work (and shamanism, its more consuming and nonconsensual subcategory) from other intense spiritual practices is the personal quality of the relationship the spirit-worker has with the spirits and deities around them. We might be lovers, lackeys, diplomats, escorts, adversaries, advocates, servants, tools, protectors, and pupils all in a single week, depending on who we encounter. To my mind, it is the way a spirit-worker relates to the spirit world that makes her/him a spirit-worker, more than the tasks of healing, divination, or trance. The distinction of spirit-worker relies on our connections to the spirits and these relationships can take many forms, especially when those relationships involve love and devotion.

Several models of devotional relationship are described in mystical texts, and we find them appearing in the lives and practices of modern spirit-workers as well. The deity may be a parent and the worshipper a child; the child looks to the parent for wisdom, guidance, and protection while the parent provides love and discipline for Their child. Many, if not most, modern spirit-workers receive their lessons directly from the spirits and deities they work with and this teacher/student relationship can be very close; as emotional closeness grows, the student learns deeper and deeper lessons. Some of us are engaged in sexual and romantic relationships or even marriage with spirits or deities; we love Them, open our homes and hearts to Them, give Them presents, miss Them when They're absent, and happily share our days (and nights) with Them. We are devotees, consorts, and spouses to Them, offering ourselves without reserve and accepting Them fully, the same way we are embraced.

It also isn't uncommon for some spirit-workers to be servants or slaves to their Gods; the god-slave phenomenon is attested to in many ancient writings. To an observer, this may look like a poor basis for a devotional relationship, with the deity benefiting at the spirit-worker's expense. For those who are in such a relationship, the reality can be quite different. While it may be a painful role to become adjusted to, it has a unique form of ecstasy and connection with the divine; the spirit-worker is made into the custom tool of the Gods, responsive and open to Their presence. It should not be disregarded. Besides, those who actually find themselves in this position will not be helped by being told that this form of spirit-relationship isn't valid, or doesn't (or shouldn't) exist.

Parent and Child

What often comes to mind when conceiving of deity as a parental figure is the Judeo-Christian God the Father. This particular Parent has a rather tumultuous relationship with His children, but it has endured and continues to flourish. The counterpart to God the Father and His often misunderstood role in His children's lives is the Great Mother Goddess described in Neo-Paganism. Her figure derives from historical sources, but these days it has a uniquely modern twist. Usually this Goddess is thought of as a loving, nurturing figure that is universal and available to all; on the other hand She is sometimes treated as a blessing-dispensing vending machine. Speaking from personal experience, I believe that there is a great She in the Universe, but I don't think She is the doe-eyed wish-granter some Neo-Pagans would see Her as. Mothers give their children what they need and sometimes children need to learn difficult lessons.

Relating to a deity as parent may bring up painful associations in the hearts of some worshippers. Histories of abuse, neglect, or absence have to be confronted when they arise in they course of this relationship. Perhaps there is the unconscious expectation that this divine parent will behave similarly to the mortal parent, or make up for what the mortal parent did not give them, or the devotee may find themselves revisiting unfortunate behavior patterns of their own. In more positive cases, the presence of divine parents helps ease the scars left by the mortal ones, or at least creates new ways of thinking about parental influence.

Whatever painful inheritance has been given by mortal parents and caregivers, it's possible to receive a joyful inheritance from divine parents as the relationship grows and deepens. For better and worse, we receive some of our self-image from the person or people who raised us; we are told our value and worth from a young age. If that self image has had the effect of limiting our growth in negative ways, it has to be undone before more positive growth can replace it. Divine parents, with greater patience and insight than mortal ones, are faced with the difficult task of helping a worshiper build up a distorted self-image into something that is more healthy and honest.

The deity-as-Parent model can exist on a huge scale, with the mortal child positioned in miniature next to a huge, galaxy-sized Parent. This can be a very comforting position to occupy, as if one is held in infinitely safe arms. Total acceptance is offered here and deep healing can happen. No matter our tantrums and mistakes we can expect to be held again, but perhaps not before being disciplined. Even this discipline can serve as a comfort; our actions do matter to our Parents, and we are not forgotten.

An interesting (though rarer) devotional model that exists next to deity-as-Parent is deity-as-Child; in this model the devotee is the parent and the deity is their Child. This dynamic is experienced, for example, by those who love the infant Christ or young Krishna. People who encounter deities this way find themselves inspired to love with the pure devotion and care of a parent. Parents often describe their children teaching them about themselves most of all, so it's not surprising that those who relate to a deity as Child find the experience highly revealing.

Teacher and Student

Many religions consider deities to be master teachers who share instruction with those mortals who demonstrate themselves to be open and prepared for inspiration. Jewish mystics study their holy books and Shaivite renunciates practice austerities to receive wisdom. Many scriptures are considered to be divine revelation, with God as the author who teaches the correct way to live and the deeper truths of life. Shamanic traditions often credit a shaman's instruction to spirits and deities in addition to any lessons given by a human mentor. As spirit-workers, especially those of us who are mostly (if not entirely) spirit-taught, the model of deity as Teacher and devotee as pupil is not hard to see.

Since our culture does not make any allowance for emotional intimacy between teachers and students, it is may be difficult to see exactly how this is a devotional relationship. However, emotions loom large when we are dealing with deities. For the mystical student, the pursuit of hidden wisdom is as ecstatic an endeavor as the devotee's pursuit of love.

The deeper we delve into our personal emotional landscape, the more we come to know about ourselves. As devotees, we are challenged by our Gods to love all sides of Them, but to do so we must in turn confront and accept all sides of our own nature. There is much that we bury behind habit, addiction, injury, social protocol, and ideas of "rightness", and stripping those barriers away can become a difficult process ... as difficult making the sacrifices necessary to become closer to our Gods. These processes are intertwined. We may abandon one type of worship for another, leave behind a home or relationship that is holding us back from our spiritual work, or give up the security of familiar surroundings in order to progress in the direction the Gods demand of us. Simultaneously, there is an inner road that must be walked; we can move to a new home but if we don't move our heart at the same time, we don't actually make progress. If we continue to hold onto bitterness over a past that we willingly sacrificed, the sacrifice was not well made. If we take up the discipline of a spirit-worker but don't remove the destructive habits of falsehood or addiction, then the discipline we display has no substance to support it through hard times. In spirit-work, no part of our nature escapes examination by the Gods or by ourselves. We must be willing to study our inner voices, read our actions line by line, and teach ourselves our own hidden mysteries.

Master and Servant

Several spirit-workers see themselves as a servant or slave in relation to their Gods, and their devotion is expressed as service—service to the deity and service to a community. Serving a community is an important, even essential, component of spirit-work. Even those who serve spirits more often than people experience this; by seeing to the well-being of local spirits, the people who live in the vicinity are benefited as well. Those who serve a human community through group or one-on-one work have the opportunity to extend their dedication to the Gods to the world around them.

Service is also an important component of renunciate and devotional lives. Selfless service—service done without asking for a reward, done for the greater good, or done out of love and dedicated to a deity—is a noble goal. Granted, there are examples of service done in the name of a deity that further political rather than spiritual goals, but I hope that those who practice service can recognize the difference.

Spirit-workers are not isolated entities; we are all part of greater communities through service or association. One of the distinctions that makes a person a shaman depends on their enforced service to a particular community. Other spirit-workers may find themselves given to a community as well. Service to people need not take place only in the context of a formal community; unless the spirits have expressed specific restrictions on what work should or shouldn't be engaged in, we are free to improve the world around us. For example, volunteer work provides ample opportunity to help better the lives of others, and donating time or money to charitable organizations is a good way to express gratitude for the riches in your life.

Sometimes deities want more than just service from us. They reach to exert control over every aspect of our lives, dictating how we eat and dress, where we live, and what jobs we can hold. Choosing not to heed Their instructions or trying to ignore Them altogether brings disastrous results. In these situations, the Gods don't resemble the benevolent or cheerful beings others report Them as being; They can be domineering or even angry. Instead of willingly taking up a path of service, a spirit-worker is forced into compliance, if only to escape further correction.

Descriptions of these experiences tend to be met with static—the person is insane or begging for attention, they're being deceived by a spirit masquerading as a deity, they have horrible self-esteem and need psychiatric help right away, they should be ashamed of themselves. But it happens. It's real and it's terrifying. Through no great fault of their own, a person can end up as what can only be described as a slave, the property of a deity.

To those who are involved in Master and servant (or slave) relationships with their Gods, devotion as such many not ever enter their minds. Ancient tribal spirit-work has a long history of relationships of an involuntary nature, and this extends to some modern-day spirit-workers; we don't choose what spirits and deities we work for and nothing we do manages to rid us of Them. We may be pulled into servitude entirely against our wishes and it's only through hard lessons and a short leash that we learn to walk the line. God-slaves experience fear and face trials that other devotees may not. The Gods can be stingy with affection towards Their tools—we may not ever know They're happy, only that They are not unhappy. There can be precious little comfort or safety in this station; our fragile mortality is used to demonstrate Their control of our lives, and our dedicated efforts meet with little acknowledgement. How can we learn to love in such a harsh and demanding relationship?

The Gods do not drive us to become anything we don't have (at least theoretically) the ability to be. Whatever we are, we are because we have the capacity for it, and in spirit-work no capacity is left unexplored. We are required to fully be everything we are; any part of our nature that is left closed or ignored is a part that is closed to the influence of Those we serve and unavailable to the people we aid. Learning to come to terms with this unpleasant process of exploration could well be an essential element of fully accepting the path of service.

If being a spirit-worker has taught me anything, it has taught me that the more power you have, the greater the requirement that you use it in service of others. I believe the same rule holds true for the Gods. They are not the ultimate rulers of the universe; They are bound by rules and consequences as well. They, like us, are tools of deeper forces and have Their own service to give. We may be kind to or dismissive of the spirits that occupy the tools we use in our work, but we should never forget that we rely on them; they are not required for us to function, but they help extend our reach further in aid of others. So do we for the Gods.

I think we come to mirror our Gods in many ways, especially as we become ever closer to Them. In a sense, we come to embody our Gods by serving Them and doing Their work; this embodiment is a deep form of the connection sought by mystics, which makes God-slavery into a decidedly mystical path. For example, deities like Hela, the Norse death Goddess, provide a great service to humans (as well as to other beings); those who find themselves close to Her in whatever way will find themselves providing service to humans (and others), as well. Hela does not discriminate between age, class, ability, gender, or even whether you are human or not. She accepts all and welcomes all at the table where She feeds the dead. So if a person comes to me marked for assistance, I am required to help them regardless of who they are. In mirroring the acceptance and service of our Gods, we perform the mystic's duty of drawing the worlds close together.

Romantic Love

Perhaps no other form of relationship has produced such an emotional outpouring as the romantic relationship. Mystics throughout history have related to the divine as Lover; in their writings the deity is described as a partner in a passionate romance. The mystic longs for the Beloved, is sad at being separated, and celebrates moments of intimacy. Many of the ecstatic Hindu poets chastised their Gods (often Kali or Krishna) for being far away. Other writers urged people to hear the call of the divine, to leave their empty lives behind and become intoxicated with love and reverence.

The idea of deity-as-Lover is often regarded as threatening. In other commonly found relationship models there is a clear hierarchy in place where the deity is the more distant partner, but n romantic love the deity is as often the pursuer as the pursued. Spirit-workers who experience this pursuit are very familiar with the tenacity a deity can exhibit in Their courtship.

In all models of relationship we are able, to some degree, to perceive something of the inner heart of these Goddesses and Gods. Through Their association with us, They reveal Their strengths and weaknesses, Their flaws and vulnerabilities. By drawing us into such close proximity They allow us to see something of who They truly are. This is probably most evident in romantic relationships since the deity may abandon the pretense of divine grandeur (except to use it as a seduction method). They want. They need. Need is part of every relationship we have in our lives, including those we share with our Gods. When the hierarchy of Parent/child, Master/servant, or Teacher/student is missing, we encounter the Gods' needs in very immediate ways.

Spouse and/or Consort

It can be very surprising to find oneself the object of a deity's affection. They may sweep us off our feet or They may show darker and more intimidating sides of Their natures, forcing the awareness of Them deep into us; in many cases love and terror go hand in hand and the more we fear, the deeper we love.

In coming to terms with the reality of a deity's courtship a choice must be made between love and what holds us back. We may be bound by fear, doubt, or disbelief but if we love more than we fear we can choose to love in the face of that fear. Choosing to love doesn's make the fear or doubt go away; we must continue to face it by making that choice over and over again. Making this choice involves a great deal of bravery every time it's made. There are questions—what if I'm wrong, what if I'm mistaken, what if I will hate it in time? We can't know the answers to these questions; instead we can only dare. Love is never safe.

This continual exercise in bravery by daring to love in the face of potential failure is an important component of faith. Faith is not the absence of doubt—faith is accepting doubt and continuing to trust anyway.

There are other obstacles involved. First, it isn't always clear what They want. Many Gods (and Goddesses) are notorious for wanting a good time and we may fear assuming too much in accepting Their affection. Most of us have no context for being in love with the divine, at least not in the immediate way They are encouraging. As we fall in love with Them, our preconceptions about ourselves are sure to be challenged. Deities have a habit of drawing hidden or buried parts of ourselves to the surface, then romancing those parts right along with the rest of us.

Once we choose to receive love and give love in return, we begin to accept the relationship the deity is offering us. We make a place in our hearts for it, reaching whatever conclusion we must in order to calm our rational minds into accepting what seems so improbable. We have to make a place in our lives as well. Maybe there is an existing relationship that must be cut off or at least be made less significant. Maybe we have to honor our Beloved on certain days or wear certain items of clothing or jewelry for Them.

An important element of embracing a deity out of love is allowing Them to be who They want to be, not who we expect or want Them to be. A married man who takes a mistress may do so not just for sexual gratification, but because he desires a place where he doesn't have to be the stern, strong provider all the time. A consort or concubine of a deity offers Them a place to unwind and be Themselves; consorts see unexpected sides of the Gods—playful, loving, vulnerable—that the vast majority of worshippers never guess at. Seeing the Gods with Their hair down, so to speak, can be startling. Deities rely on a consort to be discreet and sympathetic to Their needs. In return, a consort can receive the love and favor of deity, and a companion and confidant of their own.

Marriage

The term "sacred marriage" can refer to different things depending on the context. It can refer to the coupling of a ruler and representative of a deity, such as the ancient Sumerian kings and the priestesses of Inanna practiced. It some magical traditions it refers to ritualized sex between people. Sometimes the term refers to celebrations honoring the marriage of deities. Those who discuss sacred marriage in terms of devotional work usually refer to the union of a deity and mortal who have made vows to each other as spouses. This union is regarded as a marriage, the same as exists between people who love each other and desire to be together for life.

Sacred marriage meets with at least as much scorn and disregard as God-slavery does. It is inconceivable to the majority of people that anyone would or could have such an intimate relationship with a deity; the love and loyalty that exists is ignored or made fun of. The mortal partner may be accused of delusion or arrogance—after all, only kings and heroes have the personal attention of the Gods. In spite of these accusations, most God-spouses don't claim any particular greatness (and are often privately baffled as to what attracted their Spouse to them in the first place). We are simply passionately in love with our Gods and have been offered a unique and precious choice.

Becoming a God-spouse (or spouse to a spirit) is not a decision lightly made. It can't be undone with a simple trip to the county courthouse. Taking a deity as Husband or Wife alters your fate in permanent ways, tying your future, past, and potential to that deity. Fortunes rise and fall together, and the luck or fortune of the God is shared with the mortal, for good or ill. Your life ceases to be your own in the sense that you are the only one contributing to it. Instead, you and your Spouse live a shared life created by the effort and attention of each partner.

The rules of partnership can vary a great deal depending on the deity and the person. Some deities are happy to allow Their mortal spouse to be involved with human partners and may be instrumental in locating a "consort" for them. The deity may support or even demand the mortal spouse take a lover, even going so far as the nudge the emotions of those involved in order to achieve that end. On the other hand, it's not unusual for the deity to be very possessive of their mortal spouse and drive away any person who gets too close. If the mortal partner already has a spouse, They may allow that relationship to continue or They may demand Their spouse leave that partner (or create circumstances that end that relationship). The needs of the deity aren't the only ones taken into consideration. The mortal spouse may not be happy sharing romantic love or sexual favors with anyone except their divine partner, so the deity might encourage that exclusivity.

A God-spouse faces many difficulties. Being apparently single in a culture that practically demands a person be in a relationship is not easy; not having your marriage recognized as legitimate does not make things easier. The vast majority of spirit-workers struggle financially and some God-spouses will only ever have a single income; their Partner will certainly lend assistance but the security of a second paycheck is sorely missed. While living alone may be emotionally fulfilling for some, difficulty such as illness and injury, or even inconvenience like car trouble, is faced alone. For all the closeness of · the relationship, God-spouses still experience limitations in how well they can perceive their Beloved. We struggle with feelings of loneliness and isolation, particularly when our Partners are absent for a time.

The divine half of these marriages also experiences difficulty. They must sacrifice for the needs of the relationship too, and face the reality that They cannot be with their mortal partner as They desire to. Gods tend to be fascinated by the mundane lives of spirit-workers anyway; even the minutia of a God-spouse's daily routine takes on importance to their Husband or Wife, and They want to be as much a part of that as possible. Even though our hearts are fully devoted to Them, our busy lives sometimes demands that we divide our attention; the Gods we love dislike this as much as mortal partners dislike having their Spouse away on business. Deities can experience anger and jealousy, and sometimes require reassurance of our affection. It can be easy to forget that the divine partner in sacred marriage needs to be reminded of our loyalty, but the needs of each partner are often surprisingly similar.

There is great truth in the saying that tells us the more we love, the more we are able to love. Sacred marriage is not the self-indulgent practice it is accused of being. God-spouses strive every day to be more open to their Gods, and ideally we then carry Their presence into the world with us. By making Them such an integral and intimate part of our lives, we create a space in this world for Them and we can share that presence with others. Like anything else, we get better at loving the more we practice. Sacred marriage offers an arena for practice that is lifelong and deeply personal.

Not all devotional relationships are so easily categorized. Some relationships involve features that are defy easy classification or involve so many nuances that describing the relationship is impossible. Sometimes a deity is like a muse, inspiring us to create; a beacon that, through our creation, we chase. There may be a depth of love and intimacy that mirrors that of marriage, but that does not have the same romantic features. And then there is union, that mystical moment when all labels are stripped away entirely.

In all the relationships we share with the Gods, They become vulnerable to us. They may never show it, They may deny it, but it is true. Deities are driven to seek us out by the same nameless force that pulls us away from complacent lives and into lifelong sacrifices to see Them more clearly. We pray to Them, yearn for Them, gift and cajole and praise Them. They enchant us, capture us, pursue, aggravate, and entice us. We meet the Gods in tumultuous, emotional spaces where we are all equally captivated.

Finding a Form

A devotional path always finds expression. Devotees evidence their path in the way they dress, behave, and move through the world. Even though the relationship we share with the spirits is largely a private matter, we are still moved to give it a physical form. Evidencing passion in a tangible way is deeply fulfilling and provides a way to examine our feelings in new ways.

This emotional outpouring often takes the form of artistic creation. We write about our Gods, or create visual works of art depicting Them. Beautiful objects are created for Them or with Them in mind. Music, poetry, and performances are dedicated as offerings, as are other forms of physical activity. Inspired to know Them better, we look through historical texts, study religion and lore to discover more clues about Their nature. As spirit-workers, of course, our single greatest devotional expression is service.

In art, the word "medium" is used to describe the material a work of art is created in, but medium has another meaning referring to a substance that allows energy to flow through into something else. A medium joins two worlds, providing passage between. When we actively express our devotion, we take on the role of a medium, connecting our world to that of the wights, and our inner world to our outer world.

When creating something artistic, the act as well as the resulting product can be a medium. Writing is a perfect example of this. Those spirit-workers who express their devotion in writing take part of the world of the Gods and express it in a language that can be shared with this world. Writing can function as a way to move information between the worlds, and this exchange can happen again each time the text is read. When we read lines that were written centuries or even millennia ago, we take part in a dialogue between the world of the writer and our modern world.

Keeping a journal is a good way to establish a conversation with yourself. Journaling of any kind lets the writer move between the worlds of their conscious and subconscious, emotional and rational minds. A spiritual journal is useful for recording observations and practices, and is an effective tool for considering new ideas. When a journal has an emotional focus, feelings—of confusion, passion, trepidation—are explored in a safe way. Through writing, new aspects of emotional experiences are uncovered. Over time, it's possible to see the changes in one's emotional state and this can lead to a greater willingness to admit certain truths.

Communication is a very intimate experience; even when we are communicating with ourselves, giving a voice to our devotion can be a challenging task. We take a risk by writing anything down or by speaking up. What might be dismissed in our heads as madness or simple fancy takes on serious weight when it is introduced into the physical world. The situations that make sense on an emotional level lose all meaning when put into words; some things exist beyond expression, and trying to pin ecstasy down with letters is often a futile effort. That doesn't stop us from trying. It is gratifying to see and hold the physical proof of those precious emotions.

Art is another tangible way of bringing the Gods into our lives. Whether our subjects are our deities or not, what we create when we feel inspired by Them becomes a testament to the effect They have on our lives. We can create in honor of Them, or for Them. All creative efforts can become devotional projects, whether we paint, sculpt, draw, compose, or create electronic media. Creating art is a good way to embody emotions in an abstract form. Similar to the magical techniques of "loading" an item with energy, objects can be imbued with emotion; emotions are also energy and feeding our emotions into creativity gives a physical form to what we were feeling at the moment of creation. Whenever we see or touch what we created, we recall exactly what we felt. Not everything we create is durable or meant to be kept, though; many artistic projects are made to be sacrifices and by destroying, abandoning, or just releasing what we have created we hand it over to the Gods. Our emotions and desires are served up to Them and our efforts illustrate our dedication.

The creative process is an absorbing, intoxicating space to inhabit. When it grabs us the only thing to be done is to give in; if not, we risk losing it. When the rush is over, the process plods along as we hope for another dose of inspiration. This artistic ecstasy is considered to be a divine gift, which gives a further dimension to the art being created. We create for the Gods, but also thanks partly to Their influence. There is an analogy between creating a work of art and creating a devotional life—both involve inspired obsession surrounded by a lot of hard work and love.

Craft differs from art in that craft usually fulfills some useful purpose whereas art may exist for more abstract reasons; often these two elements are combined, creating items that are functional as well as beautiful. Many of the tools used in spirit-work are a result of personal craft; since this work tends to be idiosyncratic it is up to us to customize our tools to meet our unique needs. Even those spirit-workers who don't consider themselves to be in a devotional relationship with their Gods can create tools as a way of expressing dedication to their work. Certainly there's more pleasure in working with a lovingly-made tool than one that was created with little concern. Making tools or other objects for our practice may be a necessity, but it need not be drudgery. These tools will house spirits who have agreed to work with us, so the attention paid to creating them is a way to respect and thank those spirits.

Not everyone expresses themselves artistically. Many spirit-workers give their devotion active physical expression. Our physical bodies are the repository of every experience and feeling that has flickered through our lives; we are made of memories. As we shape the body through physical work, we uncover layers of personal archaeology. Memories may have been forgotten by the conscious mind, but so long as we have our bodies, those memories live somewhere. Activity doesn't have to take place in a health club or gym—yoga, dance, tai chi, dramatic performance, martial arts, even vigorous sex are examples of physical devotional activities. More mundane activities—jogging, walking, cycling—can take on a devotional dimension when performed with deliberation. The act itself can take the mind to a deep transformative state and in that stillness we can experience precious moments of union.

Using the body itself to express artistry blurs the lines of artist and creation—dance, for example, can't be separated from the dancer. Only a body can make dance happen and dance can't be drawn out to exist in a remote form. Through physical work, our devotion becomes integrated into us on more than emotional levels; devotion becomes embodied in our frame, living, breathing, and growing with us every day. Physically expressing emotions drives the awareness of the devotional path deep into the body, where it stays and lives like an invisible tattoo.

Disciplining the body to rigors of sustained activity is a process that pares away the unnecessary. Just as the emotional component of the devotional path burns away mental debris to make room for love to expand, the physical component of the devotional path refines our bodies so that we are more closely aligned with the object of our attention. In a sense, we have to prepare our bodies to receive the physical part of devotion, and that usually means serious housecleaning. Even then, the required conditioning itself can be understood in the language of the devotional path. In the process of burning through the obstacles living in our bodies, more fully able to inhabit our bodies and, by extension, our physical lives. As we become better connected to our bodies, we become better connected to this world and aware of the connections that form an unseen net all around us. The devotional path is based on relationship, so in the process of refining our physical embodiment one has to learn about all the physical relationships we depend on. Diets are often challenged; we aren't able to take for granted the ways in which Earth and its inhabitants support and sustain us. We have to face painful issues such as histories of abuse, physical health problems, sexuality, gender identity, and addiction. The physical aspect of the devotional path is as rigorous as the emotional and mental ones, and just as important.

Some mystic paths downplay the importance of the body in favor of refining the mind. Contemplation and renunciation may work well for some, but my own work on the devotional path has led me to a love affair with Earth and with myself as part of it. My devotion has become integrated into my physical self; I am as aware of it as I am of any other part of my body. Coming to terms with my physical nature has given me new insight into myself as a whole, and led to new ways of understanding devotion.

As was mentioned in the previous chapter, the search for knowledge can take on a mystical dimension. This quest can be fueled by our longing for the divine; by searching for mysteries it might be possible to perceive more clearly the design of the Gods and see the universe through Their eyes. So we study. We search books ancient and modern and compare notes with other seekers; over time, wisdom is revealed through contemplating and mediating upon the words. This process can reveal allegory for the life of the mystic and their striving to see the world in new, deeper ways. These mystic texts often have multiple layers of meaning and, as these layers are discerned, the seeker comes to know themselves in more meaningful ways, as well.

The recitation of a prayer or passage of text can serve as a meditative exercise, bringing the attention into a finer focus. While short prayers and holy names can be recited on prayer beads, contemplating a longer passage creates a sustained prayer that transforms the perspective in the same way that ritual does. It's possible to combine the recitation of prayer beads with the contemplation of a text; inspiration comes in many forms and getting to know a prayer both through recitation and through contemplation is sure to bring insights unique to each approach.

Many traditions have used prayer beads as a focal point for meditation and worship. In recent years, many spirit-workers have adopted the practice of using prayer beads and dedicating them to specific deities or groups of spirits. Holy names or short prayers are recited on each bead, which are strung together on a cord, usually in a significant number or multiple. I have heard four levels of recitation described, which progressively integrates the prayer into increasingly subtle levels of awareness. First is verbal recitation, which brings the process by bringing the prayer into the physical world. Second is whispered recitation and third is mental recitation; both of these levels begin to integrate the prayer on a person's emotions and intellect. The fourth level is automatic recitation; at this point the prayer has become integrated into all levels of a person's awareness and being. They have repeated their prayer so often that their mind begins reciting as soon as they see or pick up the beads. Recitation can continue even when doing rhythmic, repetitive activities like walking or washing dishes.

Prayer beads are a form of pattern magic. Pattern magic is significant because the entirety of the magical dynamic is embodied in a single element; a mantra is itself but it's also every mantra that has come before it or will follow after. Using prayer beads creates a vast store of energy that can be tapped during recitation, or channeled into other endeavors. Pattern magic is powerful on many levels.

Observances play a role in the devotional life of worshipers. Many spirit-workers perform daily altar devotions in addition to observing holy days throughout the year. Connecting to a significant date through remembrance and observance creates a chain that reaches across the material and subtle planes. Celebrating holy days unique to our traditions reaffirms ties with those who have come before us, letting us draw on ancestral strength as well. Like a spring wound tightly into a spiral column, the years revisit their previous position, but are never exactly the same.

Daily observances are formed into a pattern like beads on a string— individually a single day may not mean much, but when counted all together the time spent in daily meditation, prayer, and celebration is turned into a powerful force. Repeating actions create mental triggers that help return us to the same emotional space each time they are performed. This is a basic component of ritual work; with practice, executing any part of ritual or energy work becomes second nature and little effort is needed to achieve the desired end. So it goes with daily devotions and other observances made on a regular basis. They become more powerful the more often they are performed; eventually the pattern becomes self-perpetuating and we are caught up in the momentum of that pattern. We can't help but do our daily devotions. Often these daily devotions serve as an anchor through hard times when nothing else can be counted on for strength. The investment made into establishing this habit results in a momentum that can carry a flagging spirit through difficulty; there have been many times when I couldn't have made myself do my daily devotions on my own, but the habit was so ingrained that I was able to do them anyway.

The most significant way that spirit-workers express devotion is through work. While we may not be able to avoid the work, our mindset can transform our normal function into an offering given out of love. Since our entry into a life of service is not always voluntary, transforming that suffering into sacrifice—making our pain holy—is one of the greatest challenges a spirit-worker is likely to face. Without that transformation we risk turning our unhappiness towards those we serve and even other spirit-workers.

The notion of a community made of spirit-workers and shamans seems to be an entirely modern concept created by our ability to communicate over great distances with ease. We are able to network with others like ourselves in a way never before experienced in human history, and some have attempted to form communities bound together by common experience. For those of us involved in such communities, it may be tempting to see ourselves more in terms of those than of the community we serve, especially if we have little firm idea about what specific community we belong to; humans are social animals so it's natural to want to be around others like ourselves. It's important to remember that we draw from a well that is filled with what we contribute to any community we claim. Focusing only on the suffering we experience rather than the equally important joy may create a return of the same from the very source we desire to find strength in. This means that all those spirit-workers we communicate and interact with are benefited when we uncover joy.

Service is, by its nature, work done with intent. We expend energy and create new lines of intent and possibility in the universe, and energy runs along those lines. Through service, we become connected to other people. As isolated as spirit-workers may feel from the rest of society, our function drives us to create connections, however fleeting, with many people. Those lives we touch are not isolated, either. We affect change in their lives and if the work is successful and our clients do their parts, they carry the positive effects of that change to others they encounter. This may sound like a very trite rehashing of familiar ideas, but creating these new chains of potential may serve deeper purposes for some spirit-workers.

While some spirit-workers had children before entering the job full-time (or were able to gain reprieve to care for young children), others never had the opportunity to create families through reproduction. There seems to be a higher percentage of childlessness among spirit-workers in general. Having this option absent from their lives certainly suits some, but others must spend a great deal of time weighing the loss of the children that might have been.

Some writers credit those people whose gender identity or sexuality didn't lead directly to procreation as the reason that culture was able to develop past simple survival. Religion, art, and medicine all advanced because there were some people who had time that would have otherwise been taken up with rearing or providing for children. These people were sometimes responsible for taking in the community's youth and equipping them with the skills needed for adulthood; they were teachers and mentors. To me, this is a way for us "intermediate types" to effectively reproduce; I believe there is relevance in these queer mysteries for spirit-workers in general. While not all spirit-workers are destined to be teachers as such, we still have the ability to create change in the world by guiding and influencing others. Service is a way to enter the future as surely as we would through the vehicle of a child we raise and love. Many spirit-workers may be genetic dead ends, but that does not prevent the creation of an inheritance of information and action.

Like parenthood, spirit-work throws us into sacrifice for another's sake. Both states can't be fully understood except by those who live it; both can potentially catch a person unaware and will certainly change their life forever. Both are also largely thankless jobs, unappreciated by those very ones we do our best for. The similarities continue: some people have children without emotionally becoming parents; some spirit-workers become so bound up in their own suffering that it creates problems when it comes time to interact with those they serve or with other spirit-workers. Both parents and spirit-workers experience joy and pain in equal measure and must choose which to focus on. We may never be sure we've affected the best change, but if we're lucky, maybe we'll get a "thank you".

Crafting our practice with care and love does something to ensure that we pass along our best to those we encounter, whether they are formal clients, other spirit-workers, or casual acquaintances. Certainly when the lessons are coming fast and hard it's difficult to think about crafting anything at all; the love required for our work has to be developed the same way we develop it for the spirits. Sometimes the process is easy, sometimes it's hard. No relationship exists without trials, especially not the relationship we have with something as cussed as a spirit-worker's calling.

Evidencing our devotion to the spirits and to our path is a small way to make our mark on the world. For those who don't belong entirely to this world, the opportunity to make a change for the positive serves an important psychological function. Our work hasn't amounted to nothing, even if our names are forgotten. Our struggles have been for a greater good, even if our lives pass into oblivion. For the time that we dwell on this world we can express love in tangible, potent ways. By doing so, we create new lines of potential that can eventually be realized as transformation.

Part 2:

Forging the Tool

Bumps in the Road

No relationship is without its pitfalls, no romance without its conflict. No matter how deeply devoted we are to our paths and our Beloveds, there will come times when despair, anger, sadness, confusion, and doubt overwhelm. We lose sight of the road that seemed so clear and begin to question even those convictions that seemed unshakable—is loving the spirits all that important after all? What is gained from all this sacrifice? Why do the Gods bother with me? What is the purpose of this service? Why do I serve at all?

If there were no need for us, it's safe to assume the Gods would not bother spending so much attention on us—and some of us require a great deal of it before we learn our lessons. But why? We aren't necessarily obligated to assume the Gods' side in whatever cosmic enterprise They're involved in, no more than They are obligated to root for our home team. In every life of service we must search for an answer to the question "why do I serve?"

Sometimes the Gods share with us Their reasons for acting. According to Them, there is some dire need for us: action must be taken, knowledge must not be lost, balance must be maintained. As agents of the larger universe, the Gods are charged with keeping everything in harmonious balance. This isn't always the peaceful sort of harmony we think of, but rather a harmony in which no one force overpowers any other. That, so far as I can figure, is Their official job description (your opinion will certainly vary). We assist Them in this by attending to the details in a way They can't. For all Their might and wisdom They are not human. They aren't really able to appreciate our perspective any more than we can grasp Theirs. By working together we can each achieve more than either could on their own. The Gods need us.

We also need Them. It's been my observation that many, if not all, spirit-workers have a need to serve. If a spirit-worker doesn't have that need in the first place, they develop it later on as their well-being becomes tied to whether or not they do their job. A need to serve shouldn't be interpreted as a sorry, groveling desire to debase oneself (though I believe that this need, unfulfilled, can be expressed in unhealthy ways). A need to serve is a desire to make a difference, to be an active rather than passive presence in the world; it is a desire for meaning in a life where little meaning may be apparent. For others, the love of our Gods is reason enough to serve; we love Them and desire to selflessly express that love by helping improve the world around us. These people believe in the power of hope, love, and faith and try to inspire these qualities in others so that all are better able to face the difficulties of life.

Many mystics who practice selfless service see their God in the face of every person they help; the presence of the divine is seen even in places of suffering and squalor, and those who serve do not turn away, seeking instead to love all faces of their God and to extend love and mercy to all in need. When I began working one-on-one with people in my local community, I was startled at the humility and compassion I experienced when confronted by their need. I felt blessed to be in a position of service. To me, service is not something I "do" but something I allow to happen; through hard work and dedication I hope I am able to allow the correct aid to come through me and into the world. There is infinite need but also infinite compassion available. Through those who selflessly serve, the worlds meet in a continual dance: need inspires compassion, which in turn opens a person more to the divine.

There will always be a greater need in the world than there is ability to fill it. I feel that those people with a need to serve, a need to fill need if you will, are specially placed to help counter the larger need. Those who chose a life of service may do so out of a conscious or unconscious desire/need to serve. Those who are compelled to a life of service may find that they are deeply satisfied because of it. Need may be the only thing that fulfills need. Of course, a life of service is a difficult one. Often we can't see the larger importance of our small and seemingly pointless efforts. What does it matter to the Gods' work that I never eat meat again? What higher purpose is served by me wearing this or that color, or by moving to another state or country? Why do I serve those who don't care if I live or die? What difference does talking to that person make? We may trust that these things do have purpose—to increase mindfulness, discipline, and responsibility; to influence just the right person in just the right way; to help clear the accumulated psychic ill of a culture; to serve the spirits so they are not neglected or forgotten; and so forth. But sometimes—or frequently—questions and doubt cloud that deeper faith.

Questioning one's faith is unavoidable. Indeed, it probably shouldn't be avoided. Through wrestling with these questions we come to our own conclusions about the purpose and meaning of our work. We may get by for a while on the Sunday School level answers to these questions, but eventually we must earn our own answers. It is a good and important thing to trust in Those we serve, and continue to work even in the face of this doubt; this is part of faith. Another part of faith is that which we have earned through wrestling with doubt and arguing with our hearts. Which side will win? The rational mind that longs to kiss off the greater work and go back to a predictable life, or the irrational (but all too real) experience that there is much, much more to this world than we could have ever imagined? If experience wins out over rationale, we must face the rather difficult conclusion that not only are these things very real, but that we have a very real place in them. The spirits know our names and where we sleep at night. This can be hard to come to terms with, especially when held up against a former life that was mostly normal.

Even if we were able to go back to that life, would we? Some spirit-workers or potential spirit-workers seem to have that option. I'm reminded of that scene from *The Matrix* where Cypher is willing to sell out his friends and everything they have fought for just to go back to sleep. It comes off as a selfish and ultimately doomed act, but I'm sure we can all relate to that desire.

We spirit-workers have something rare. We have the Gods' attention. The spirits notice us when we speak to them. Our world is at once bigger and smaller than most people could even image. We are forced to know ourselves on a level even the best psychotherapists couldn't help us achieve. The biggest questions in life are answered for us, even if those answers aren't very comforting. Moreover, if we manage to find answers to those questions for ourselves in addition to whatever answers the Gods have given us, we have a rare and powerful thing—unshakable faith in our purpose.

Faith in the importance of service is a hard thing to earn; it is something that I will certainly struggle with in new ways my whole life. I question my God' wisdom and sometimes wonder if They improvise as They go along. I wonder if, for all Their insight, They have questions, too. It doesn't seem unreasonable that They would. If anything, this line of thought is comforting; perhaps I don't face my questions alone. I can accept Their fallibility with more understanding and accept Their patience with me, instead of ignoring it with protests of "You just don't understand." If the Gods sometimes wonder about Their effectiveness, then my hard-won faith is doubly sweet because I know it is not my triumph alone.

It is all too possible to feel exploited in this work. We give and give, either willingly or through pressure, and are shocked to find that we have been plundered on levels we didn't know we had. Deep and secret parts of our hearts get trampled on in a rush to get us to act according to divine will; we feel cheated, tricked, and used. Even going into a devotional relationship with the knowledge that wights are dangerous doesn't keep us safe; we still have our hearts on the line. Sadly, it is only natural that innocence ends. The Gods will not allow us the illusion of thinking of Them only as benevolent guidance counselors, and the spirits don't like being cast as the cheerful helpers one might find in an animated fairytale movie; They will make sure we don't think of Them as one-sided. This, too, is a teaching tool. Deities especially test boundaries, pushing and demanding of us in order to get us to stand up and find our limits. On the other hand, not everyone is allowed to set those limits. It may be equally important for one person to learn to submit and surrender as it is for another person to learn to say no. The Gods know who we are, and what works best for each of us.

Suffering is an all-too-familiar feature of the lives of many spirit-workers. We might have suffered on our way to this calling, and we are likely to experience suffering all throughout. Some suffer the unique pain of deconstruction or shaman sickness, or experience a loss of fortune, health, and/or mental stability. It can be all too easy to get stuck in suffering, especially for those in the throws of deconstruction. However, suffering serves a valuable purpose. It is one of the only ways to build deep compassion, something all spirit-workers need. When confronted by another's need, be it the loss of their luck, health, sanity, family, or cherished dreams, we have to understand the these experiences in a personal way as well as know ways to relieve them.

Pain forces a rather self-centered focus to develop, but it can also force us to reach out and beg for help. The experience of suffering can demand that we become open and vulnerable to others. If we are too closed or too controlled a dose of insanity opens us right up. If we have trouble letting people into our lives, a debilitating illness can force us to be dependent on others (and then accept with grace the requirement that we later depend on others as per the rules of our spirit-work). Personally, the only way I have found to cope with the emotional toll taken by deconstruction is to become open to love and compassion. Even if it is safer and easier to withdraw and be angry, I allow that to pass and focus on compassion. (Usually I have to do this multiple times.) I found purpose in suffering when I allowed it to help me open to love—the love from and for my Gods, and the love I have for the world. Through love, I make suffering into a sacrifice.

Cultivating gratitude is another way this suffering can become sacrifice. Find one thing to be grateful for, or one thing you appreciate. When pain is particularly intense this isn't easy, but find just one thing—the color of the sky, the grass pushing through the pavement, the richness of physical senses, the recollection of a favorite song—and be grateful for it. Anything at all. Then do it again. Do it as often as you can, especially when the pain starts to overwhelm. Remember to thank the Gods. Too often people get into the habit of asking for things in their prayers or conversations with the Gods and forget to follow up with any words of gratitude. Forgetting to thank the spirits and deities for what they give us narrows our vision and prevents us from seeing exactly what they do for us. The service we offer to them isn't part of a one-way transaction. We receive efforts in turn, whether we recognize them or not.

In addition to having compassion and gratitude, it is important for spirit-workers to find peace. All too often, peace isn't readily found outside ourselves; for those who serve dark or chaotic deities, peace may be a rare thing. So we have to give it to ourselves instead. Peace is more than simply the absence of strife or violence; I believe peace is the maintenance of Right Action and the encouragement of the same. Right Action helps us discern when we need to take and when we need to give, when to speak and when to be silent. Peace helps to bring an awareness of our actions and the consequences of our actions (whether we opt for peacefulness or not).

The harsh use we may be put to is not the sum total of the life of a spirit-worker, though it may sometimes seem to be that way. I believe that by engaging in this work we gain the very tools necessary to allow us to continue in it. It can be difficult, if not impossible, to glimpse the treasures amid the toil, but there are many valuable things we can gain for ourselves even as the pieces of our lives slip further and further away from our control. Peace, gratitude, faith, and compassion are inexhaustible, and do not depend on the spirits' generosity. We are not put into debt by sharing these things with the world; if anything, we become richer for the sharing. In the moments of darkness when it feels like we have given and lost all that we have to offer, these are the infinite fonts that will continue to nourish us.

Love Comes Full Circle

Why do we love our Gods? Because it is in our nature to do so, because we can't do otherwise, and because through loving them we come to more fully be who we have the potential to be. Just as the process of falling in love with the divine parallels the process of falling in love with our spirit-work, the answers to the first question apply equally to the question "why do we serve?": because it is in our nature to do so, because we can't do otherwise, and because through embracing service we become who we have the potential to be. We can relate to the spirit-worker's calling in the same ways we relate to the Gods in our lives. This work may be like a parent, guiding us through life and providing necessary (if unpleasant) rules to live by. It may be like a master, waking us in the middle of the night to see to the needs of an honored guest. This work may be a teacher, allowing us to be by turns amazed by our ignorance and awed at our ability to learn our lessons well. And, of course, the work may be a lover whose strong arms hold us close and never let go; we belong to this Beloved and we come to perceive its private heart. In these ways spirit-work becomes devotion.

The transformation of spirit-work from vocation to love affair is the process of months and years of effort dedicated to removing the emotional obstacles that prevent us from losing ourselves in the work. After all, we can't fully fall in love with another person without taking a risk and passing that point of no return. Until we can approach spirit-work without reservation it will remain a conditional occupation—only when we have time, only when we are forced, only when we have a client in front of us, only when there is a clear objective in mind, and only when we risk losing nothing in the process. Ideally, over time, spirit-work will become something we are, not just something we do. Like love, our service will refuse to stay compartmentalized, given attention only when it is convenient for us. It will follow us around, appearing at unexpected moments, sometimes when we would have much rather been doing something else. This happens not just because spirit-workers have a very long, involved to-do list, but because we fulfill the function of spirit-worker just by showing up. On my way to do completely unrelated tasks, people have unexpectedly met me; they will tell me how they needed someone just then and wasn't it lucky that I happened to be there? In these cases I am often valued not for what services I could potentially render, but for my presence. The people I encounter don't want me to do anything; they just needed to know that there was help available in the cold universe and that they were not forgotten or alone. Sometimes, just showing up and standing around fulfills the job in front of us, whether or not we were even aware of a job in the first place. Spirit-work is not limited to what we do; it is very literally who we are. It happens whether or not we are aware of doing anything special, or of doing anything at all. Integrating and internalizing spirit-work until it becomes a seamless part of the self's entirety is part of what happens when spirit-work ceases to be a part- or full-time hobby and becomes an expression of devotion to the world.

The power and secret of the devotional path is that it has more than the power to take us close to the spirits. It can bring us to a loving, compassionate relationship with the world itself, renewing a jaded sense of altruism, and removing the barriers that keep us apart from other people and from the whole of the natural world. It is possible to love this world and all that lives and dies in it with the same intensity we love our Gods. One of the pitfalls of the mystic's path is to become so singularly focused on the otherworldly that only disdain and pity are left for the worldly. Early on, this was something I ran the risk of; my relationship with the world and with myself was so flawed that I treated my relationships with the Gods as a way to escape paying attention to the gritty, mundane world. Hela solved this problem by placing me squarely in the service of people. If I wanted to serve the Gods (and I did), I would do so by serving humanity. It's not easy; my commitment to this devotional life is tested continually. What keeps me coming back to this practice is my unshakable faith in the power of the devotional path; the simple fact is that using the tools of this path consistently yields positive results. I have come to find gratitude for being placed in this service because it offers me yet another way to fall in love; just as I can help bring the love for my Gods into my work with people, so too I can bring the love I have for this world into my relationships with the Gods.

In working for and loving Loki, I have come to appreciate the game the Hindus call *lila*. *Lila* is the love-play between *maya*, the power of illusion that is personified as a Goddess, and worshipper. For most Hindus, *maya* is something to be overcome through sacred observances, austerities, and the power of the Gods; illusion is what keeps us on the wheel of reincarnation, continually accumulating karma, or action, that must be undone. For some others, *maya* is the veil Shakti (the feminine power of the universe) wears; *maya* gives a face to the faceless and a name to the nameless. Because we are all in on the joke—that *maya* is illusion—we are free to play with it, safe in the knowledge that it's all undifferentiated energy. *Lila* is a game of falling in love over and over again with the many faces of the divine. How many disguises can the Beloved wear? Are we observant enough to recognize Them no matter what? Deities can present themselves in a myriad of ways. In fact, the world itself can be considered just another aspect of the divine (since everything is made of primary source material anyway), so falling in love with the world is a natural aspect of the deity-centered devotional path, and not as radical as it may sound.

We begin with only ourselves and our yearning for the divine. Once our search leads us to the Gods and once we have found our Beloved, we extend ourselves out to Them and draw Them close to us. Discovering Their many faces leads us back to the world and the process begins again. This continual interplay bridges the worlds and brings them together. Loving the world and loving the self as part of the world brings the devotional path full circle and will lead to unexpected facets of practice.

It is said that spirit-workers and shamans live in two worlds, that they straddle the dividing line and live in the shifting, dangerous boundary that separates this world from others. This was true historically and it is true today. The strain of living in two (or more) worlds is a unique one and may not be something that everyone becomes totally accustomed to. Since devotion brings the worlds together, I believe it can lessen the strain and allow us to move back and forth with greater ease, since in reality we are not going very far at all.

Like spirit-work, the Heartroad is more than something you do. It is something you are, and becomes something that happens as naturally and with as little thought as breathing—and like breathing, can become more focused and powerful with deliberate practice. To internalize the devotional path you have to fall in love with it, too. It will become less an "other" and more of a "self." Our relationships with the Gods and with our work are bettered for finding love.

Like love, this work is never easy, but it can be sweet. Talk to the work. Love it. Taste it. Take it into your arms. Picture your challenges as fears to be comforted, and soothe these fears with love. See the people you are set to work with as a myriad of disguises your lover wears in an endless game of hide-and-seek. Make an altar for your tools and honor their spirits because they help you draw closer to your lover, mistress, and teacher. Take refuge in the relationship.

Learning to love this gift from the Gods and spirits is a lifelong challenge. We may mourn the plans that had to be abandoned when we were compelled down this path and we may struggle with the desire for a normal life. Overcoming these regrets, even for a while, is an offering we can make to show gratitude. In the moments you love your job and love your life, thank the Gods for it. Thank yourself for your ability to walk this path, and thank the work for the opportunity it offers you. This too is an expression of love.

Epilogue: Lilahava

When I fell in love with Loki, I was a woman. I had the body, name, and experience of a woman, and never questioned this identity. I fell in love the way a woman falls in love—deeply, passionately, holding nothing back. Enthralled by love, I touched my deepest heart and felt myself more feminine for this honesty. After a conflicted childhood and ambiguous adolescence, I finally glimpsed who I would be as an adult woman. I placed that future woman in the hands of my Beloved, because He had led me to her.

That future was only an illusion. Like the other illusions I've held up as reality, it had to be ripped away. I was not a woman. I never had been. My body had changed—it spoke to me in new, foreign words. My name was taken—it dissolved like a sandcastle in the surf. I didn't recognize my voice or the possessions that filled my home. My closet was full of clothing I couldn't wear and my reflection, about which I had always been ambivalent at best, was now starkly alien. I no longer experienced myself as a woman and it was painful to reconcile a history that predicted a radically different pattern than that which I was suddenly experiencing. Nothing in my life had prepared me for this transformation and no evidence had suggested that my life would begin again. Lacking any past, I couldn't glimpse the future.

The presence of the Gods withdrew from my life and I found myself terrifyingly alone. My God-husband of less than a year was beyond my sensing and the Goddess whose hand had shaped me was silent. I was left alone to stumble through my days in a body that didn't want to cooperate with my brain; I was forced to become aware that I had always severely lacked a sense of my own physical embodiment. I had ignored and denied my physical state, allowing illness and bad habits to settle into my flesh. I was often crippled by arthritis, I ate poorly, and I treated my body badly; all this revealed a contempt that I never knew I had. My mental health was revealed to be as poor as my physical health, and deteriorating rapidly; I had to face the bad behavior my unacknowledged mental problems had spawned. All distractions were removed and I had to learn to live with myself for the first time in my life.

For months I suffered, sick with the knowledge that I had mistreated the relationship I treasured most in the world. Feeling empty, I had selfishly sought to fill myself with love, thinking that my need for that love would justify its continual offering. The harsh treatment I had endured in service to Loki weighed down my heart and prevented me from loving from a place of true generosity; I sought to punish Him with my fondness instead. Loki's absence was constantly on my mind; without His voice and presence my life was suddenly very empty and quiet. I tried to love with the same feminine emotions I had experienced with such depth and intensity, but the fire that had lit my spirit had gone out. The way I loved had depended on my sense of myself; as I further became a sexless, nameless living dead thing, I struggled to find a heart to love from.

My desire to reconcile my relationship with Loki proved to be the incorrect focus, or at least it should haven't been my only focus. Instead of making a hard examination of what life as a transgendered person meant, I fled from the dysphoria and knowledge that I would never be a woman again. Understandably, I was in mourning, but my focus on loss prevented me on facing the life I had been reborn into. I went back on prescription antidepressants after having been free from them for the first time since puberty. Stress, denial, and a sudden change in prescriptions landed me in a hospital. I had been given exactly a year to come to grips with my new identity, and I had made slow progress. It took a strong message, but I finally decided that I had to accept the reality of my circumstances, and that meant learning to love again.

This wouldn't come easily. If I couldn't love as a woman, what could I love as? I was not a man and my sense of myself as a third gender person was barely beginning to take shape. Surely I had to be someone before I could love; I had to have some source to pour emotion out of, some container I could offer myself from. If I was no one at all, what shape could love take and what term would describe the relationship? The answer came simply. If I didn't know who I was, I would love as whoever I might become. I would love from every potential identity I may come to someday embody. Not being a man, perhaps I couldn't love with a man's heart, but I could try. If I was no gender at all, perhaps I could love as a human being, as a mortal whose heart belonged irretrievably to the divine. I fell in love again and in doing so, I shifted. I became more than what I had been and my identity flickered like a rapid slide show, showing me all possibilities and combinations. I was all these things and none of them, but that didn't matter so long as I could love. Love, then, was my true identity.

My husband came back. Safe in this love, I finally allowed myself to explore my new life. I changed my wardrobe and learned a whole new kind of bravery. My emotions fluctuated wildly, lines of identity crossing and doubling back, over and over each other until I became tangled in myself; Loki was always there, helping me work out the knots of another adolescence. He became She, and She became wife as I became husband. I discovered the feminine heart of my spouse in ways I hadn't seen before, and felt my own self-knowledge become deeper through His revelations. I became increasingly adept at riding His shifts, the radical and subtle. He remains patient with me, finding joy in my complexity the same way I revel in His.

Through this odyssey I have learned that I don't need to be a woman to love deeply and I don't need to be a man to love intensely. All that Loki demands is that I love Him most of all, with loyalty and joy, without reservation or self-deception. With this message in mind I am free to explore who I am and who I may become safe in the knowledge that no matter how shifty I am, I will never lose this love— not its gift nor its reception. I will never become someone my beloved spouse fails to recognize and He will never wear a disguise I can't fall in love with all over again. All this shifting has revealed new ways to love and new insights into each other. It's became a game between us— *lilahava*, the exchanging of clothing so as to love from a new point of view.

Following me through the struggle of falling in love with Loki again was a relationship with Hela that had been forged even before my lifeoath to Loki had been given. She had always been encouraging, supporting me through the highs and lows of being a Loki's woman. Hela had been a sister and aunt, an exacting teacher and formidable guardian. I had trusted Her absolutely, but fought hard when it became evident that I would work for Her instead of Loki; where He had owned me, now She did. I couldn't speak to Her or tolerate having Her stand close to my most private feelings; Her presence was intrusive and I bitterly resented Her.

Coming to love Hela took years of effort; I would stride forward then become upset and back away again. I knew that I would be unable to walk Her path if I didn't love Her—it is not in my nature to be motivated by many things except the desire for intense connection— but I couldn't get through the walls I had carefully constructed to keep everyone except Loki away from my heart. When I reached a breaking point of being unable to turn away any longer but not being able to let Hela fully into my life, I finally turned to the spirits for help. With the aid of some flower spirits, I cast a love spell on myself during a seven-day ritual/ordeal cycle. The process broke me open and after it was over I was at last able to allow myself to become vulnerable to Her. Now, I am at peace with Hela's presence. She is part of me. Once I was able to stop hating myself, I could stop hating Her hand on my life; as I have come to love and accept myself, I have come to love and accept Her.

"Love," Loki once told me, "is not a finite thing." These words have become the mantra that describes my relationship with Hela; I love Her in complex, intimate ways and I continue to expand to encompass all the ways in which She loves and treasures me. I no longer feel divided between my Gods, at war with myself because I felt unable to give myself fully to one without depriving the other. Over time, I have become big enough (or perhaps small enough) that I can easily hold both Loki and Hela in my heart, and be held by each of Them. It has been Hela as much as Loki who has led me towards some peace with my new self. She finds my jigsaw-puzzle faultlines beautiful and offers my in-between identity absolute acceptance.

I am still only newly formed. As of this writing, over a year has passed since I put on new clothes, and a little more than that since Hela gifted me with the name I earned. I have spent this time trying to puzzle out the existential questions of my purpose and necessity; why am I the way I am, and why now? I am slowly learning the Mysteries appropriate to my masculine and epicene genders, and navigating the rough waters of a strange Gods-given adolescence. I still reel at sudden shifts and try to be compassionate towards the rebel body I find myself at odds with. There are many hard questions about my future that are difficult to contemplate but that continually demand observation. Love—the desire for and the experience of—has been the single constant thread through this life and the one that came before. I have loved myself through destruction and renewal, through dark nights and lonely days, and I will continue to love as I step towards the future.

The devotional path has proven to be more resilient than any part of myself; it endures where I have failed and carried me when I lagged behind. I have complete faith in this path; it transformed as I transformed, and has acted as a loving (if exacting) mirror to explore myself. I would not have my husband, my spouse and partner, without this path, but more importantly I wouldn't have myself. I found that he Heartroad does more than lead us into the arms of our Gods: it can lead us to enduring, unshakable self-love. The pattern holds true whether we direct that love towards the spirits, towards our work, towards the world, or towards ourselves. It will follow us along every bend the road of our lives may take and it will lead us into perfect, blissful, loving union with itself.

It is my honor and pleasure to have fallen in love with love itself. I would choose no other vehicle to carry me through this spirit-worker's life and out into the world. I would choose no greater calling than this, no more worthy endeavor. Love has led me to my Gods, to my work, to the world, and to myself. For this, I bless it.

About the Author

Silence Maestas is a writer, teacher, priest/ess, spirit-worker and spouse to Loki; he has been involved in pagan devotional work for more than ten years. In addition to years of personal exploration, Silence has been trained in Wiccan ritual by the Order of Our Lady of Salt in Salt Lake City and has served as seid-worker in Asatruar kindreds. This is his first book.